Migration Nation

Australia's Multicultural Food

Sally Cowan

Migration Nation: Australia's Multicultural Food

Text: Sally Cowan
Publishers: Tania Mazzeo and Eliza Webb
Series consultant: Amanda Sutera
Hands on Heads Consulting
Editors: Sarah Layton and Tania Mazzeo
Project editor: Annabel Smith
Designer: Leigh Ashforth
Project designer: Danielle Maccarone
Map illustrations: Petros Bouloubasis
Permissions researcher: Lumina Datamatics
Production controller: Renee Tome

Acknowledgements
We would like to thank the following for permission to reproduce copyright material:

Front cover: Rawpixel.com/Shutterstock.com; p. 4: History collection 2016/Alamy Stock Photo; p. 5: (top) Australian Natives' Association/wikimedia commons; (bottom) MalikNalik/Shutterstock.com; p. 6: KGPA Ltd/Alamy Stock Photo; p. 7: (left) Chronicle/Alamy Stock Photo; (right) The State of Queensland; p. 9: Mitchell Library/State Library of New South Wales; p. 10: (top) Liliya Kandrashevich/Shutterstock.com; (bottom) Viktor/Adobe Stock Photos; p. 11: alexzrv/Shutterstock.com; p. 12: (left) Tim UR/Shutterstock.com; (right) The Sydney Morning Herald/Fairfax Media/Getty Images; p. 13: (top) Alexey Stiop/Shutterstock.com; (bottom) warat42/iStock/Getty Images; p. 14: MilanMarkovic78/Shutterstock.com; p. 15: (top, p. 32) DesiGNProtic/Shutterstock.com; (middle) Sinisa Botas/Shutterstock.com; (bottom) SolStock/E+/Getty Images; p. 16: (top) Dorling Kindersley ltd/Alamy Stock Photo; (bottom) Stephen Dwyer/Alamy Stock Photo; p. 18: Peter Ptschelinzew/Alamy Stock Photo; p. 19: (top left, back cover) Pixel-Shot/Shutterstock.com; (top right) Stephen Dwyer/Alamy Stock Photo; (bottom) Amr/Adobe Stock Photos; p. 20: (left) sathit/Adobe Stock Photos; (right) Dragonimages/Dreamstime.com; p. 21: (top) Jina Ihm/Alamy Stock Photo; (bottom, p. 3) Алиса Королевская/Adobe Stock Photos; p. 23: (left) cfresh okra/Adobe Stock Photos; (right) Nataly Studio/Shutterstock.com; p. 24: (top) Afromeals/Shutterstock.com; (bottom) bonchan/Shutterstock.com; p. 25: (top) Marcos Elihu Castillo Ramirez/iStock/Getty Images; (bottom) Friendly Studios/Shutterstock.com; p. 26: (top) Adam Hanley/Shutterstock.com; (bottom left) Yagya Parajuli/Shutterstock.com; (bottom right) Indra Saputra Ahmadi/Shutterstock.com; p. 27: Imgorthand/E+/Getty Images; p. 28: (top) (title page) Maskot/Alamy Stock Photo; (bottom) jax10289/Shutterstock.com; p. 29: Chun Ju Wu/Alamy Stock Photo; p. 30: LuckyBusiness/iStock/Getty Images.

NovaStar

ISBN 978 0 17 033507 2

Cengage Learning Australia
Level 5, 80 Dorcas Street
Southbank VIC 3006 Australia
Phone: 1300 790 853
Email: aust.nelsonprimary@cengage.com

For learning solutions, visit **cengage.com.au**

Printed in Malaysia by Papercraft
1 2 3 4 5 6 7 29 28 27 26 25

Nelson acknowledges the Traditional Owners and Custodians of the lands of all First Nations Peoples. We pay respect to Elders past and present, and extend that respect to all First Nations Peoples today.

Contents

Moving to Australia

Have you ever wondered what it would be like to move to another country? Or what you might miss from home if you did?

Migration is when people leave their homes to move to a new country and build lives in a new community. Australia has a long history of **immigrants** coming from around the world, and there have been many larger **waves** of migration in recent years.

Since the end of **World War II** in 1945, people from nearly 200 countries have come to live in Australia. The first migration waves came from wartorn Europe after World War II. More waves followed towards the end of the "White Australia" policy in the 1960s and 70s. Other waves of migration have continued from the early 2000s to the current day. Over decades, this migration has changed Australia in many ways.

Immigrants from Europe headed to Australia in large waves.

From the time that **British** people arrived in Australia in 1788, Australian communities have become much more **multicultural**. Immigrants have introduced many new things like different languages, traditions and foods. If you enjoy eating foods like pizza, noodles and falafel, you have migration to thank for it! Before the 1950s, most people in Australia had not heard of these foods.

Why "White Australia"?

The White Australia policy (1901–1975) was based on the **racist** belief that non-white people were **inferior** to white people. The newly created Australian government of the time wanted to limit non-British immigration to Australia and prevent non-white people from moving to Australia at all.

Pizza is a food enjoyed by many people in Australia.

Food Before World War II

Immigrants in Australia have always brought some of their favourite foods from their previous countries with them. It's comforting to eat the foods you are familiar with, especially when everything else about your new home seems quite different.

When British people came to **colonise** Australia in the years after 1788, they brought familiar foods with them from home.

People settling in Australia set up farms to help grow their own foods.

At that time, the First Nations peoples in Australia ate a variety of foods that were **native** to their environment. But British people didn't recognise the foods in their new environment and continued to eat what they were used to.

In the mid-1800s, thousands of Chinese workers came to Australia temporarily as diggers during the gold rushes, and **Afghan cameleers** arrived to help the British explore the outback. But because many of these people were not allowed to stay in Australia or bring their families, the **culture** and foods in Australia remained largely British until after World War II.

Chinese diggers work during the Victorian gold rush of the mid-1800s.

Afghan cameleers help a British woman explore the Australian land.

First Nations Foods

First Nations peoples in Australia hunted animals, like kangaroo and wallaby, and caught fish, turtles and other seafood. They also collected and grew a range of plant foods, including fruits, roots, herbs, nuts and seeds. Many First Nations peoples still eat these foods today.

Post-World War II

After World War II, the Australian government wanted to increase Australia's population to help build up the **economy**. The government believed that a large population could also help to defend the country in case of another war.

Although large numbers of British people immigrated to Australia at this time, there were still not enough people coming from Britain to meet the government's needs. So, for the first time, thousands of people from mainland Europe were given the chance to immigrate to Australia. The first waves of migration came from eastern and southern Europe. These immigrants would gradually influence the kinds of foods that people ate in Australia.

Migration Waves from Eastern and Southern Europe to Australia

After World War II, many people came to Australia by ship from countries in eastern and southern Europe, including Poland and Italy.

The Eastern European Wave

After much of Europe was destroyed in World War II, it took a lot of time to recover. Food and shelter were hard to find in the ruined cities. Millions of **refugees** couldn't return to their homelands, especially in eastern Europe. They became known as displaced persons, or "DPs". In the years after the war ended in 1945, thousands of DPs came to Australia. They were the first wave of permanent immigrants to come and live in Australia who weren't from Britain.

MIGRATION FACT

More than 170 000 displaced persons immigrated to Australia between 1947 and 1953.

A large group of displaced persons arrives in Australia by boat.

Immigrants to Australia from eastern Europe often found the food in their new country too plain. They wanted to eat food with familiar flavours from their homeland. Spices like paprika, dill and caraway seeds were essential for their traditional meaty stews – one of the most famous of which was called "goulash". But these ingredients often weren't available in shops.

Some immigrants managed to **import** these ingredients, and they opened shops to sell them to other people in their community. Vegetables such as beetroot and radish were not commonly grown in Australia, so migrants began growing them. Other ingredients, such as poppy seeds and sour cherries, were also imported to bake into traditional cakes and desserts.

goulash

FOOD SPOTLIGHT: Kugelhopf

Eastern European cake shops became popular in the 1950s. Some of these shops still sell the famous "Kugelhopf" (pronounced *koo-gul-hop-ff*), which is a rich, flaky cake with chocolate or poppy seeds swirled through it. It's made in a round tin with a hole in the centre.

People in many countries in eastern Europe, such as Poland, Hungary and the former **Czechoslovakia**, had a tradition of making pickled vegetables using cabbages and cucumbers. This helped fresh vegetables last longer, usually by soaking them in water containing salt and vinegar. The pickled vegetables could be stored and eaten during long, cold European winters. Although Australian winters were much milder, the familiar flavours were a comforting link to a distant homeland. Today, it's easy to find these ingredients in supermarkets around the country.

Pickled vegetables are common foods today. Many people still prepare the vegetables themselves, but they are also sold in supermarkets.

Many immigrants also soon adopted Australian methods of cooking. For example, barbecuing became popular in the warmer Australian climate.

The Southern European Wave

In the 1950s and 1960s, southern Europe was still slowly being rebuilt after World War II. Thousands of Italian and Greek people immigrated to Australia looking for better living conditions.

Many southern European immigrants came from warm areas of Europe, close to the Mediterranean Sea. They were used to eating the fresh ingredients that grew well in this region, such as eggplants, broccoli, tomatoes, zucchinis, olives, grapes and fresh herbs. They also used another ingredient that was essential in Italian and Greek cooking: garlic. At this time, most Australians still ate British-style foods, and they believed that garlic was too strong to use in their cooking.

MIGRATION FACT

From 1945 to the 1970s, almost 380 000 Italians and more than 160 000 Greek people immigrated to Australia.

An immigrant family arrives in Sydney aboard an Italian ship, *Napoli*, in 1950.

garlic

Before leaving Italy and Greece, many immigrants had tended fruit and vegetables on their own small plots of land. So, when they could not find these foods in Australia, they began to grow them in their own gardens. Some newcomers set up larger **market gardens** to grow food and sell it to the public.

Today, these foods form an essential part of a healthy diet throughout Australia.

Many people grow tomatoes in their gardens.

FOOD SPOTLIGHT: Garlic Prawns

Garlic prawns are now an Australian favourite for many people! These prawns are pan-fried with butter or oil and garlic. This simple combination of flavours helped to spread the popularity of garlic in dishes in Australia in the 1970s.

Italian Immigrants

Italian immigrants also brought new cooking skills to Australia, such as the skill of making pizza and fresh pasta. Pasta could be served as a hearty meal with different types of sauces. It was a change from the British tradition of largely eating meat, potatoes and boiled vegetables.

Making pizza is fun for the whole family in many Australian kitchens.

Bolognese sauce was a traditional type of stew cooked for hours, using meat, tomatoes, onions, olive oil, herbs and garlic. Eaten with fresh **parmesan** cheese grated on top, it became widely available and popular in the new Italian restaurants opened by immigrants. The popularity of the dish spread among Australians, resulting in the quicker version of home-cooked "spag bol" that many enjoy today.

FOOD SPOTLIGHT: Spag Bol

Spag bol is a bowl of spaghetti with sauce that contains minced meat. It is quicker to cook minced meat than the larger chunks of meat used in the traditional Bolognese recipe.

Tea was still a popular drink for adults in Australia after World War II. But the Italian newcomers brought with them a love of strong coffee, made using an espresso machine. The taste for this coffee gradually spread throughout the wider population and created the coffee culture that is popular in Australia today.

Traditional espresso pots produce strong coffee.

Many people all over Australia enjoy drinking coffee together.

Greek Immigrants

Greek immigrants in Australia also opened restaurants and cafes that served much-loved Greek dishes. There were creamy dips served with a flat bread that was very different from the white bread eaten by most Australians at that time. Another popular layered dish called “moussaka” (pronounced *moo-sar-ka*) was made with eggplants, minced lamb and a rich, creamy sauce. There were also plenty of other delicious new foods to choose from, including marinated souvlaki meats cooked on skewers and savoury spanakopita pastries made with feta cheese and spinach.

These Greek dishes and ingredients have become everyday foods throughout most of Australia.

MIGRATION FACT

Today, the city of Melbourne, Australia, is home to the largest number of Greek people outside of Greece.

spanakopita

There are many restaurants across Australia that serve traditional Greek food.

No More "White Australia"

When Australia became a **federation** in 1901, a racist migration policy called the White Australia policy was made law. It was designed to favour British immigrants and prevent people from Asia, Africa and most countries outside Europe from moving to Australia.

From the mid-1960s, the White Australia policy had become unpopular in Australia. Its racist beliefs did not reflect the attitudes of the time, and Australia had moved away from accepting only British immigrants after World War II. The government still needed more people to move to Australia and help build the economy. This time, it looked for new migrants outside of Europe.

In 1973, the government, led by Prime Minister Gough Whitlam, brought in a new migration policy to create a more multicultural Australia. It meant that people from anywhere in the world could move to Australia and make it their home.

Migration Waves from the Eastern Mediterranean and Vietnam

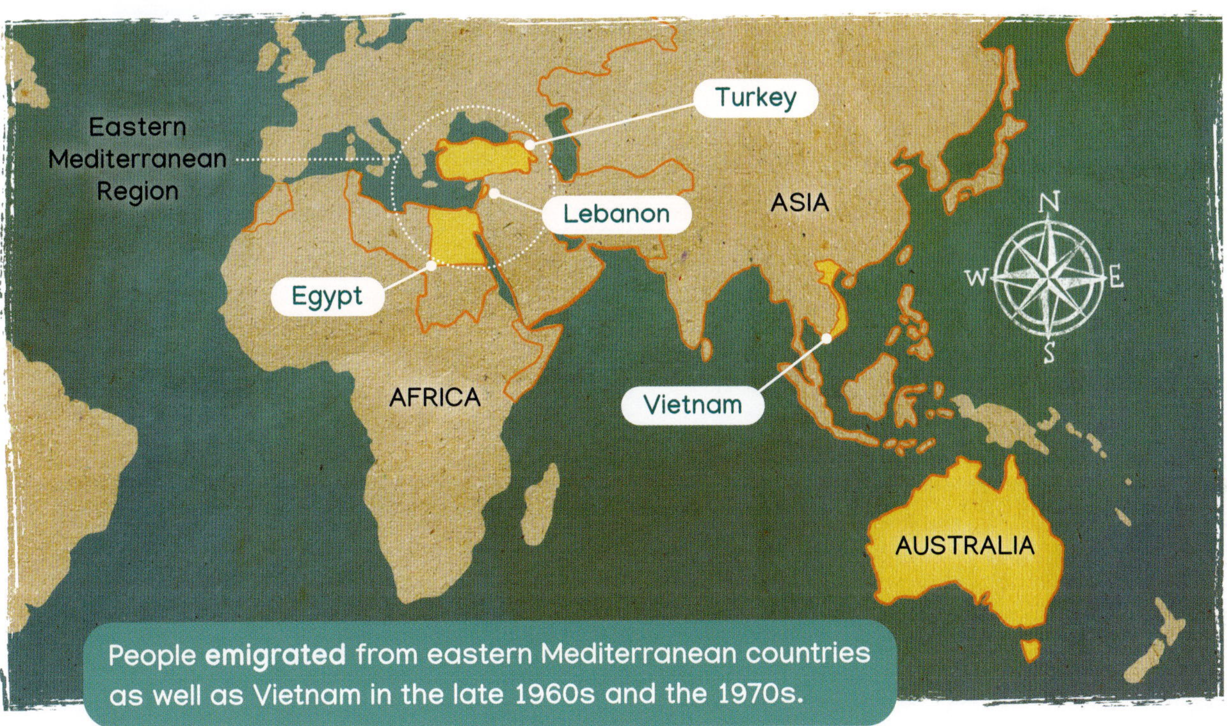

People **emigrated** from eastern Mediterranean countries as well as Vietnam in the late 1960s and the 1970s.

The Middle Eastern Wave

Turkish, Lebanese and Egyptian Immigrants

MIGRATION FACT

Between 1968 and 1974, almost 20 000 Turkish immigrants arrived in Australia.

In 1967, the Australian and Turkish governments signed an agreement offering people from Turkey the chance to immigrate to Australia. The Turkish government encouraged its citizens to leave the country due to a lack of jobs and housing in Turkey. These people became the first wave of migrants to move to Australia from outside Europe.

This woman celebrates in traditional clothing at Melbourne's Turkish Festival.

During the 1970s, the Turkish migration wave continued. People also came from other countries in the eastern Mediterranean, including Lebanon and Egypt. These people were trying to escape from war and **unrest** in their region.

In Australia, the newcomers found a wider range of food choices than those who had come in the earlier migration waves. But they still brought their own traditional foods and flavours with them, such as falafel, kebabs, hummus dip and sweet pastries. These dishes are a part of the huge variety of foods available in Australia today.

Turkish delight is a sweet treat that migrants introduced to Australia.

Kebab shops are very popular throughout Australia.

FOOD SPOTLIGHT: Spicy Falafel

This dish from the Eastern Mediterranean is made of mashed chickpeas that have been mixed with spices, rolled into balls and deep fried.

The Vietnamese Wave

From 1976, a new wave of immigrants arrived in Australia from Vietnam. They fled as refugees during the Vietnam War. It was the first time that large numbers of Asian people had immigrated to Australia.

Although a large range of vegetables, herbs and fruit were sold in Australian shops, Asian varieties of these foods weren't readily available. Many Vietnamese people began to grow familiar plants in their new home. These included bok choy, lotus root, lemongrass and banana blossom.

MIGRATION FACT

In 2021, almost 335 000 Australians claimed to have a Vietnamese background.

banana blossom

Backyard vegetable gardens enable people to grow familiar foods.

Rice, a main ingredient in Vietnamese cooking, was already available in Australia. But other ingredients like tofu (made from soya beans) and rice noodles were not. Flavourings such as fish sauce and shrimp paste were also not common. Vietnamese newcomers set up businesses to import them, and some opened restaurants and food stalls. At first, they catered for the new Vietnamese communities seeking familiar dishes from their homeland.

There are many Vietnamese fresh fruit grocers around Australia.

The Vietnamese cooking methods of steaming and stir-frying foods are used to prepare dishes with fresh vegetables, fish or lean meat. This healthy way of cooking soon spread to the wider Australian community. It's a popular option for home cooking and eating out today.

FOOD SPOTLIGHT: Pho

Many Australians love to eat pho (pronounced *fuh*) – a clear soup with noodles, vegetables and meat. It's a popular Vietnamese dish.

chicken pho

Migration Today

People from many different countries have immigrated to Australia so far this century. People have come from all over the world to live in Australia, from countries such as India, China, Sri Lanka, Afghanistan and Syria. There have also been two significant migration waves – the African wave and the Latin American wave.

Migration Waves from Africa and Latin America

People from many parts of Africa and Latin America have immigrated to Australia over the years. (Latin America is the name used for parts of South America and Central America.)

The African Wave

In the late 1990s and early 2000s, people from several African countries, including Sudan and Ethiopia, started to settle in Australia. Many of these people had been in refugee camps for years after fleeing war and unrest in their homelands. Today, skilled workers continue to come to Australia as part of the African migration wave.

MIGRATION FACT

By 2020, 400 000 people had immigrated to Australia from several African countries.

Many African migrants lived on farms in their homelands. They had planted and harvested their own food, and the preparation and cooking of food was often done together as a community activity.

Today in Australia, many people from Africa continue to work together to grow familiar fruits and vegetables in community gardens and farms. Many of the tropical crops that grow in hotter African countries, such as okra, Egyptian spinach and sorghum (which is a grain), don't grow well in cooler areas of Australia. So, people have tried growing alternative plants that give their foods similar flavours.

okra

sorghum

There are now many African restaurants in cities and suburbs around Australia. They serve a range of traditional dishes, such as fufu and jollof. These foods contain lots of fibre, vitamins and minerals that are good for healthy bodies.

Jollof is a rice dish from West Africa.

FOOD SPOTLIGHT: Fufu

Fufu is a mashed dough meal often made with vegetables such as plantains or yams and served with soups and stews.

The Latin American Wave

Many Latin American people have also come to live in Australia this century from countries in South America and Central America such as Columbia and El Salvador. Some of these countries have poorer economies and unstable governments, and people might emigrate to look for better job prospects. Many people also want to study at Australian universities to improve their job opportunities and their standard of living.

Some common ingredients in Latin food are hot chillies, black beans, tomatoes, capsicum and grains like corn and quinoa (pronounced *kin-wah*). Dishes such as tacos and burritos filled with meat or beans, spicy salsas and small savoury pastries called "empanadas" are popular Latin foods.

Tacos are popular dishes to make and share with friends and family.

FOOD SPOTLIGHT: Empanadas

Australians are big fans of meat pies, so it's no wonder empanadas are popular. These little pastries are filled with meat, cheese or vegetables and fried until golden.

beef empanadas

Modern Australian Food

During Australia's early migration waves, some Australians may have been hesitant about eating new foods like garlic and spicy falafels. But Australians have come to embrace different foods. Many Australians regularly cook recipes that come from a variety of cultures. They enjoy eating out at new restaurants and cafes that offer dishes from all over the world.

There has also been an increased popularity in Australian native foods farmed and eaten by First Nations peoples. In the early 2000s, many restaurant chefs began to add Australian native foods to their menus. Today, herbs such as lemon myrtle and native mint are more commonly sold in shops, along with chutneys and jams made from bush tomatoes or lilly pilly berries. Other common native foods include macadamia nuts, Kakadu plums and kangaroo meat.

lemon myrtle flower and leaf

lilly pilly berries

Kakadu plum fruit

Waves of migration have led to the diverse foods people eat in Australia today. In fact, with around 30 per cent of Australians being born overseas, there's no limit to the new cultural experiences Australians can enjoy together. In the future, people will continue to arrive and make their home in Australia from all parts of the world, adding to the country's wide range of delicious foods.

People in Australia enjoy foods that have been introduced from cultures around the world.

Tempt Your Taste Buds at the Night Foodie Market!

A food review by Luca

On Saturday evening, my family and I visited the Night Foodie Market in town. Even though it was chilly outside, it turned out to be the perfect opportunity to eat delicious, warm foods from many different countries.

Night food markets give people the opportunity to taste different types of food.

The fun began as soon as we arrived at the market, with a band playing Latin music. That immediately got my little sister, Ava, up dancing! The twinkling fairy lights strung around the market created a magical atmosphere, too.

More importantly for me, some delicious aromas wafted from the colourful food trucks parked around the market. Whether you were looking for kebabs, dumplings, or fun combinations like taco pizzas and **matcha** gelato, the market had lots of foods to tempt your tastebuds!

Trying all the different foods at this market was like taking a mini trip around the world! But I do suggest opting for the small plates of food, which most of the food trucks offer. That way, you can try lots of flavours without getting too full!

Lots of delicious foods from cultures all around the world are cooked at night food markets.

Apart from the food, I think one of the most enjoyable parts of visiting the market was chatting with the friendly food-truck owners. Many of them are immigrants who are keen to share stories about their homelands and their traditional recipes.

The Night Foodie Market is a deliciously special experience. I recommend it to anyone who is hungry and loves to try foods with different flavours. I've already marked the date for the next market night in my calendar, and I suggest you do, too!

There are many friendly people who prepare lots of delicious foods at night food markets.

Glossary

Afghan cameleers (*noun*)	camel drivers who worked in the Australian outback
British (*adjective*)	from the United Kingdom of England, Scotland, Wales and Northern Ireland
colonise (*verb*)	when a country takes over another country to settle its own people there
culture (*noun*)	a way of life for a particular group, community or country
Czechoslovakia (*noun*)	the old name for the two countries now known as the Czech Republic and Slovakia
economy (*noun*)	the way a country makes money
emigrated (*verb*)	to have left one's home country to live in another
federation (*noun*)	a country made up of smaller states that is controlled by one national government
immigrants (*noun*)	people who have moved to and settled in a new country
import (*verb*)	to bring goods into a country from another for the purpose of selling them
inferior (*adjective*)	not as good as something else
market gardens (*noun*)	large gardens used to grow crops for markets
matcha (*noun*)	a kind of Japanese green tea made from leaves crushed into a powder
multicultural (*adjective*)	made up of people and practices from many different cultural backgrounds
native (*adjective*)	plants and animals from a specific area or region
parmesan (*noun*)	an Italian hard cheese that is often grated and used in cooking
racist (*adjective*)	unfair towards people because of their race or the colour of their skin
refugees (*noun*)	people who have had to leave their country to stay safe
unrest (*noun*)	a state of disturbance and tension
waves (*noun*)	large numbers of people who migrate at the same time
World War II (*noun*)	the biggest international war in history, which was fought between 1939 and 1945

Index